Praise for *Retirement or a Third Act*–

Paula Black is truly a master communicator and visionary of the meaning of life. She provides a depth of self-reflection and understanding that reaches into each reader's heart, spirit and mind to self-define the journey of what is next, what is important, and how to get there. I could not put the book down once I opened the first page. A deep soul-searching experience with profound outcomes. —Lorenzo A. Trujillo, Ed.D., J.D., Assistant Dean (Ret.), University of Colorado School of Law; Affiliate Professor of Music, Metropolitan State University in Denver

Paula Black's *Retirement or a Third Act—What Will You Choose?* reminds us that a fulfilling third act that we choose —and "choose" is key—is enhanced by considering what part of our lives makes us happy today, and then our being so bold as to act on it. She outlines the homework to be done to enable us to choose wisely, and then … "Just do it!" —M. Thérèse ("Terry") Vento Pérez Art Museum Miami, Deputy Director for Legal and Government Affairs and General Counsel

Retirement or a Third Act—What Will You Choose? empowers you to move beyond the work you may have done for decades and discover those tasks that bring you energy and enthusiasm. In this book Paula Black also helps you uncover the secret to treating each day with reverence and joy. —Geraldine Hogan, retired judge; former teacher, and author of *Career Moves for Teachers and Other Professionals: Strategies for a Successful Job Change*

Paula combines part inspiration, part methodology and part love to create the perfect recipe to empower readers to take charge of their 3rd act. This book is the perfect gift for anyone who is wondering what's next or what's missing in his or her life. Its heartfelt stories, stunning photos and practical advice make it a unique and powerful tool to take charge and to rethink what is possible in this life. —Lauren E. Smith, executive & board search consultant

An exuberant examination of the possibility that you can at any time create contentment and purpose. Inspiring on every page! The book gives you the tools to stand in the present and see a meaningful future with questions that will put you into action. —James Kitchens, business owner

Paula's book, *Retirement or a Third Act—What Will You Choose?*, is a gem of a read! Funny anecdotes coupled with catchy phrases really make you stop and think about your 3rd act and what you can make it—the workbook format coaxes you to answer probing questions. It is refreshing and uplifting and provides a truly optimistic perspective on how to approach our later years in life! The pictures are beautiful and all the more meaningful because Paula took them and then shares how she has created a 3rd act of which to be envious. —Mercedes M. Sellek, Esq. Partner, Mercedes M. Sellek, PA; Founder, Ellesquire Women's Network

Once again Paula is blazing the trail for us. As she has led so many of us to robust professional practices with her coaching skills, now she leads us to a fulfilling life after we leave the practice ("Third Act"). Paula, thanks again! —David M. Rapp, Partner, Hinkle Law Firm

This was so insightful, inspiring, relevant, mind-bending (in a great way), and just what I needed to read. If anyone says they can't relate to any part of this book, then they are not seeing the big picture of possibilities. It was spot on in every way. Everything about this book resonates on so many levels and will pull you into the present and makes you think enthusiastically about the next scene in the Third Act. Loved it. —Debra Tyler, President–South Florida Division, Bank OZK

Paula Black has inspired countless lawyers to live their best lives while growing successful practices. Now she has created a workbook to help lawyers design their best "third acts," whether that means retirement, continuing to practice law, volunteering, trying something completely new, or some combination of all of the above. In *Retirement or a Third Act—What Will You Choose?*, Paula asks the right questions and provides real life examples to help us identify our priorities, make a plan and take the leap into a fulfilling third act. —Susan R. Heal, Third Act Adjunct Professor, Florida Gulf Coast University

Don't be deceived by the title Third Act. If you have been sitting at home for the last few months of this pandemic pondering the following questions—Am I living to my full potential? Am I making a difference in this world? Am I doing what I love? What would I do if I knew I would not fail?—then this book is for you. This workbook is a unique blend of provocation, inspiration, and practical application, all designed to help you unlock your passion and live life on your terms. Be prepared to be pushed way out of your comfort zone and into a brave new world of self-discovery. Paula serves as your personal guide to help organize your thoughts and goals to create a tangible plan for your future. Her vulnerability is refreshing and creates a safe space for the learner. Don't wait another minute to dig in to this workbook! —Laura Ravo, retail guru, author, and speaker.

A practical and succinct, yet powerful book. Once again, Paula Black has a captivating way of forcing me to take an important look at my life and determine how my career can support my happiness. As I look down the road, I used to wonder what was next. After reading this book, I realize I determine where I go next. —Suzanne Sarsfield Scarano, President, Forethought Marketing

Don't read this book if you are not willing to be coached, goaded, encouraged, reminded and dragged into creating your best life by a talented visionary! Paula's book gives us opportunities to pick it up, work a bit, reflect a bit and gets us moving toward our best possible third act. —Fritzi Gros-Daillon, MS, CSA, CAPS, UDCP; CEO, Household Guardians; Director of Education, Age Safe America

Retirement or a Third Act is an invaluable and highly practical guide for any senior professional who wants to take the lead in ensuring their life is filled with purpose, passion and fulfillment as they enter into retirement. The deep and meaningful questions the book invites one to consider can also be equally beneficial for those at any stage of life. Well done Paula, and thanks for your never-ending commitment to helping others create and live their best life both professionally and personally! —Gary Breininger, President, BGR Coaching & Strategic Solutions Inc.

As I start to look at my third act, I needed this perspective. It's far too easy to just follow what our parents did, even if it's not right for us. Passion for the things we love help keep us young and relevant. Thanks for the inspiration and the stellar examples to motivate! —Marty Harris, President, SEP Communications

As the "best friend" Paula refers to in her travels, I am the living example of how these questions and challenges can manifest into an amazing third act. Paula has spent the last few years working her magic during our daily chats and I am eternally grateful! If not now...when? —Laura Ralston, Director of Retail Experience, Museum of Contemporary Art, Chicago

Paula's workbook is an invaluable tool and resource for people of all ages. This excellent book shows us that we are never too old—or too young—to learn, grow, thrive, prosper and enjoy our lives. —Bruce Biltman, Esq., certified county, family, circuit mediator, arbitrator, umpire

For me your book couldn't have been more timely. As I begin to enter my third act (yes, I have a written plan!) your workbook will become my checklist. You provide such great direction and so much to think about and consider. —Edward Sachs CPA ACP, collaborative financial neutral

Paula Black's workbook is for those of us ready to look beyond who we are and consider who we might want to be in the third act. This little workbook collects the decision tools necessary to trigger action by all who turn the pages with a ready mind. —Sam Young; lawyer, investment banker and entrepreneur

I love it! Paula's workbook is inspiring and hopeful. She guides us through our multitude of excuses, life choices, and options to help lawyers navigate a transition in life. She coaches lawyers to do the thinking, the planning and then—just do it! —Sheena Benjamin-Wise, Esq., principal attorney of the Law Office of Sheena Benjamin-Wise, PA; President of Gwen S. Cherry Black Women Lawyers Association

A road map to a better balanced tomorrow. You can have it all and Paula is your guide. —Larry S. Rifkin, Esq., Managing Partner, Rifkin & Fox-Isicoff, P.A.

Paula frames thoughtful thinking, planning and the action steps to creating our best third act. The topics are relevant and most importantly for me—a timely read. —Patrick Abuzeni, MD

Paula's book is thought-provoking and offers a step-by-step process, solid observations and an easy read. It perfectly summed up the many thoughts that have been rattling around in my head as to what to do next with my career, law firm and life in this new crazy decade. A simple but powerful reminder that life is short and we should live it on our own terms. —Lillian A. Ser, Esq., Founder, Ser & Associates

Take a break from your endless Zoom meetings and depositions and read this book. Paula is great at driving her message home with an eclectic collection of quotes and her interesting life story. It will give you another perspective in these crazy times. Maybe even convince you to quit your job. —Saidin M. Hernandez, tax and estate planning attorney

It's so easy for us to lose front-of-mind consciousness and do what we have always done. Paula helps us to be present, to live in the moment and follow our own path...not the path anyone else has set for us. And she reminds us that we are more relevant and more valuable to our customers, friends and loved ones the more we are true to ourselves. Thank you, Paula! —Susan Morris, Co-Owner, Advanced Business Learning, Inc., and ABL Cyber Academy

If you are in need of inspiration and seeking new ways to understand and plan what is next in your life, look no further. This workbook will encourage you not to put the pleasures of life on hold. —Monna Morton, Vice President, Retail Property Advisors

Paula's book shows that retirement is not the end, but a milestone. Embrace the choices and opportunities you have to design the next part of your journey. Achieve new successes and savor the experiences that take you to new destinations in your life. —Marta Alfonso, Principal, Morrison, Brown, Argiz & Farra, Certified Public Accountants and Advisors

I love the way Paula's book redefines retirement. A third act is a much better way to focus on possibilities. I like the exercises that helped me think about what I want to do. In fact, she inspired me to do something with MY sunset photography. Most importantly she opened the door for me to ask myself the question—am I spending enough time with MY mother? I have taken it for granted that she is around the corner and I think we can do things tomorrow. I now realize tomorrow is now. So I'm going to have her teach me all my favorite family recipes. Thank you, Paula! —Nery Suarez, Sr. Executive Assistant

It is powerfully IN-SIGHT-FULL Timely! Practical! I loved the chapter separations, photos, and quotations. They caused me to think, and more importantly, to feel, to enjoy even more! I'm ready and living my THIRD ACT ahead of my subsequent acts. —Gilbert K. Squires, P.E., BCS, Squires International Law, PLLC

Moving from NYC to Miami was my Second Act and I thought my last, but after reading Paula's book I see I can start My Third Act. —Jill Rubin, Partner, CALAS Accounting & Bookkeeping

RETIREMENT OR A **THIRD ACT**

What Will **YOU** Choose?

An Inspiring Workbook for Seasoned Professionals

Paula Black

Copyright © 2020 by Paula Black

All rights reserved. No part of this book may be used or reproduced in any manner whatsoever without written permission from Black Box Publishing, except as provided by the United States of America copyright law or in the case of brief quotations embodied in articles and reviews. The scanning, uploading and distribution of this book via the Internet or via any other means without the permission of the publisher is illegal and punishable by law.

Please purchase only authorized electronic editions, and do not participate in or encourage electronic piracy of copyrighted materials. Your support of the author's rights is sincerely appreciated.

Published by Black Box Publishing

For more information, contact: info@paulablack.com

ISBN - 978-1-7354772-0-6 (paperback)

ISBN - 978-1-7354772-1-3 (e-book)

Cover design by: Layne Mitchell, Layne Creative Services

Interior design by: Patrizia Sceppa, Inc.

Printed in the United States of America

I dedicate this book to all my teachers, mentors, bosses, colleagues, and friends who guided me, challenged me, and most importantly believed in me. And to those who didn't believe in me—they too inspired me to push harder and find the path that would lead to success. Sometimes it's the rejection that reveals the right path.

CONTENTS

By the way, this workbook contains some cool photographs, if I say so myself. I'm an amateur photographer—it's one of my passions—and I finally found a way to play with them: INSTAGRAM! And I'm using some of them here; 70% of the photos are mine. I hope you like them.

Section ONE

Section TWO

“

Be patient with yourself.

Nothing in nature blooms all year.

paula**black**
business & professional development coach

TO BEGIN WITH

HOW WILL YOU DEFINE YOUR FUTURE?

WHAT IS A THIRD ACT?

The way that I define a THIRD ACT: Yes, technically it is the stage of life that we call retirement. But I think it is much more. Maybe we never quit working or volunteering. Maybe we are busier than we have ever been. Maybe we finally do something we have wanted to do since we were young. Or maybe we finally show the depth of love we feel for someone. As a THIRD ACT, we know the play isn't over! A THIRD ACT can be filled with opportunities to create more HAPPINESS, JOY, and FULFILLMENT in our upcoming decades based on a lifetime of wisdom.

Jane T. Smiley—my boss, colleague, mentor, and friend.

Jane posing under a painting of her when she was in her early thirties, 2010

Jane was a trailblazer; she was the first female Vice President for a Federated department store.

Jane hosting an event honoring Gloria Steinem, 1983

Jane and me at the National Association of Jewish Women luncheon naming her as a "Woman of Power," 2016

To Begin With

When I turned 50, I went on a mission to ask my then 76-year-old mentor, Jane Smiley, and her friends, "If you had to do it all over, how would you prepare for your third act differently?"

It was eye-opening, exhilarating, and encouraging. I interviewed 37 of Jane's friends, some at dinner parties Jane arranged and some over a private lunch. They were all professionals, both women and men. They were former CEOs, publishers of newspapers, realtors, retail executives, entrepreneurs, lawyers, and accountants.

A few of the answers were expected, such as, "I would have managed my finances better for retirement." But I heard one response that I didn't expect, and I heard it from every single person I spoke with. They all shared some version of the following: "I wouldn't have retired so soon—65 was way too early!"

And now, at the young and tender age of 68, I couldn't agree more wholeheartedly. Not that there is anything wrong with endless rounds of golf or bridge!

Jane is gone now, but I'm sure she would have something to say about navigating your eighties and nineties. She would look back on her life and say, "Oh, no big deal." But her life was a big deal. She was a strong woman who forged her own path.

WHAT DOES HAPPINESS MEAN TO YOU?

Bruce Springsteen said,
"It ain't no sin to be glad you're ALIVE."
Yes! I took that photo at a concert in Copenhagen.
So, what could make YOU happy,
or just "glad you're alive?"

More time with family, more vacations, more cases, better cases, more cash flow, more peace, better relationships, more fun, less stress, more love, less work, more family dinners, more exercise, more time off, more help, bigger house, smaller house, less stuff, better stuff, more time to myself, less time in the office, more time hiking, more time sailing, more time cooking, less time cooking, more time to read, more time to play the piano, more time to dance, become a judge or reinvent yourself.

Could any of these mean happiness to you? They were goals gathered from my clients. Each of them meant happiness to one of my clients and they made them all happen.

What do you want to put on your list? What would make YOU happy?

HERE IS MY HAPPINESS!

> The more a daughter knows the details of her mother's life, the stronger the daughter.
>
> —Anita Diamant
> *The Red Tent*

paula**black**
business & professional development coach

ANGELINA HELEN LUCERO

My mom has been an avid reader and a lover of movies all her life. In the late seventies, when I was a special events director for Burdines, I organized a luncheon and fashion show with Gloria Vanderbilt when she was launching her jeans line and her book, *Women to Women*. Ms. Vanderbilt signed a book for my mom. That started my mom's passion for biographies. Today she has a library of over 750 biographies.

Her movie collection is over 1,000. She has them all listed in a binder by title and by leading actors. So if we feel like watching a marathon of Robert Redford movies, we can go to her catalog and see which movies she owns starring Robert Redford.

To say my mom is organized is an understatement. All my life I have seen my mother figure out a system to do everything from managing her rental properties to her many positions at AT&T.

I love my mom and have always had a GREAT relationship with her—ever since I moved away from Denver when I was just 19, we talk on the phone three or four times a week. And I would always try to visit once or twice a year. BUT often, too often, I would make plans and then cancel at the last minute.

For example, about eight years ago I had scheduled a visit to Denver to visit Mom.

But then, one of my clients, the New York Times Syndicate, called to schedule a meeting on the very day that I had promised my mom that I would visit. Of course I had to fly to NY to meet with my VIP client. Right? Knowing Mom would understand, I said yes. I didn't even ask if it could be the following week. So I rescheduled my trip to see my mom.

Not long after that, I got an invitation to speak

at the American Bar Association Conference in Chicago—on the rescheduled date. I canceled AGAIN!

I started feeling pretty darned guilty, and reflecting on these cancellations, I realized I could have negotiated another date with the New York Times. Certainly I could not have moved the American Bar Association conference.

My mom was 78 at the time and I thought, "I have to figure out how to spend more time with her. Maybe I'll take the summer off." Who was I kidding?

"Maybe I'll have her come to Miami for the winter." She hates the heat!

"Maybe I'll start a coaching practice in Denver." DUH! So I made airline reservations for the entire year—BOOKED!

I went to Denver for her 80th birthday and announced that I would be coming to Denver every other month. I thought that declaration would be met with joyous cheers. She said, "Oh, how nice." So when I arrived the next month, my mom said, "I didn't think you would really come."

WOW! Everyone who knows me knows I'm a person of my word. If I tell you I'll be there Tuesday at 2:00, you can bank on it! But the most important person in my life couldn't count on my word. How gut-wrenching is that? When Mom said, "I didn't think you would really come," well, that was my wake-up call and a defining moment in my life and for my career. It was time for me to take responsibility and to figure out HOW to balance my work and my personal life. And that's what I'm going to share with you in this book.

Mom is now 87; I've been going home to Denver for seven years. When I land in Denver, I call her once I'm in the rental car because she wants to be on the porch ready to start our movie marathon. I arrive with the perfect movie itinerary—drama, comedy, and a good dose of tearjerker. We schedule

---

"My mother shed her protective love down around me and without knowing why people sensed that I had value."

—Maya Angelou

---

time to exit the theater for lunch or dinner, and in the interim we keep our strength up with popcorn and Junior Mints. Our record is SIX movies in one weekend and more popcorn and Junior Mints than I will admit to!

When I realized that I could integrate a coaching practice in Denver with what my heart wanted—spending more time with my mom—that set a whole new life in motion.

HERE'S SOMETHING ELSE THAT MAKES ME HAPPY, SHARING!

The Florida Bar

International Law Section Retreat

I asked the members... What are the myths that hold you back from attaining happiness in your practice?

And THIS is what a THIRD ACT looks like for me! I love speaking and giving professionals another way to look at their practice, their clients, and their life!

"Happiness is when what you think, what you say, and what you do are in harmony."

—**Mahatma Gandhi**

TAILOR YOUR
THIRD ACT
TO FIT IN

HARMONY

WITH YOUR
PASSION.

HOW DOES IT FIT?

> Happiness is not a matter of intensity but of balance, order, rhythm, and harmony.
>
> —Thomas Merton

paulablack
business & professional development coach

Work-life balance doesn't exist! It's a matter of keeping them in harmony.

I love travel, photography, music, my best friend, and working with professionals.

This one page brings all of that together for me!

TRAVEL? On a cruise in the Black Sea—
Check.

PHOTOGRAPHY? I took this photo at an outdoor concert in Ephesus, Turkey—
Check.

MUSIC?
Check.

MY BEST FRIEND? With me—
Check.

And now, I'm sharing it with YOU—
Check!

Five things I LOVE, working in harmony!

How could you make your life work in HARMONY? List your ideas.

"One day, you will wake up and there won't be any more time to do the things you've always wanted. Do it now."

—**Paulo Coelho**

WHAT'S STOPPING YOU?

FEAR?

Life is thickly sown with thorns, and I know no other remedy than to pass quickly through them.

—Voltaire

REALLY! We have ALL lived TOO long and
accomplished TOO much to let FEAR stop us.
As Voltaire said, pass through the thorns QUICKLY.

YOU CAN'T?

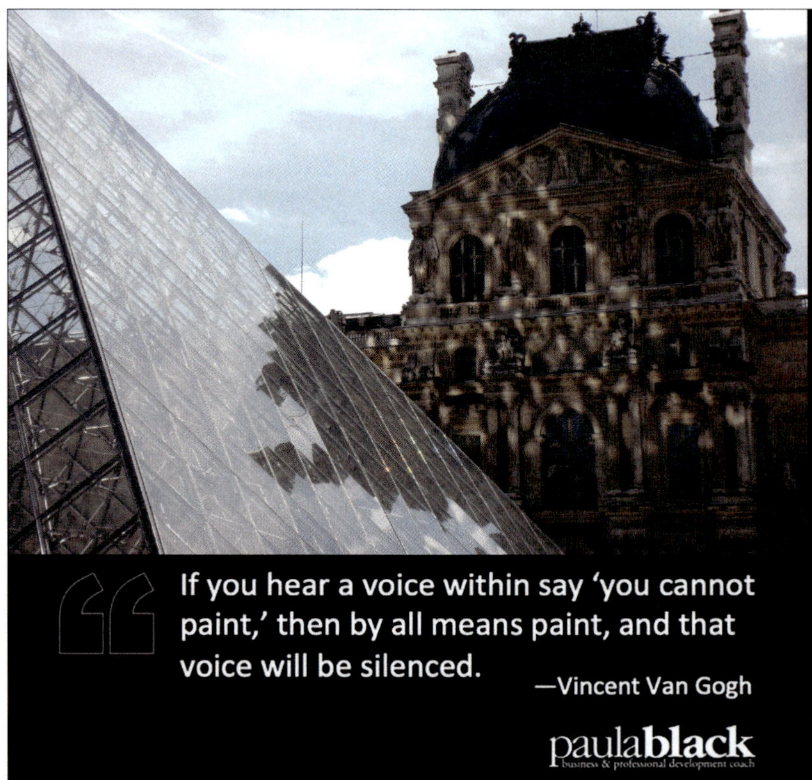

If you hear a voice within say 'you cannot paint,' then by all means paint, and that voice will be silenced.
—Vincent Van Gogh
paulablack
business & professional development coach

REALLY?

YOU have had a long successful career!

And YOU CAN'T achieve your dreams?
NONSENSE. YOU CAN!

Van Gogh knew how to silence the voice in his head. OKAY, so he cut off his ear. But the point is well taken. Don't listen to the voice that tells you YOU can't!

Consider Robert Schuller's question—"What would you attempt to do if you knew you could not fail?"

YOU DON'T KNOW HOW?

YOU DON'T know HOW?
If you are reading this book you are probably a LEARNER and PROBLEM SOLVER.
Figure it out! LET the LIGHT IN.

PERFECTIONIST?

> I never expect perfect work from an imperfect man.
>
> —Alexander Hamilton

paulablack
business & professional development coach

PERFECT DOESN'T EXIST!

No human being is perfect, nor is anything we do.

We are always a work in progress. AND everything we do can be improved. Every proposal, brief, contract, closing argument, or article.

Remember Hamilton's assertion not to expect perfection.

This is the photograph I took the night I saw Hamilton on Broadway. It was GENIUS! The lyric "I'm not throwing away my shot" resonates with me. Lin-Manuel Miranda wrote those words referring to the revolution and the opportunity to build a sustainable democracy—and I hear them as a cautionary cry to not throw away my shot at a fulfilling THIRD ACT.

What do these words mean to you?

“Don’t worry about failure, worry about the chances you miss when you don’t even try.”

—**Jack Canfield**

IF NOT

NOW

WHEN?

"I DON'T HAVE TIME," YOU MAY SAY.

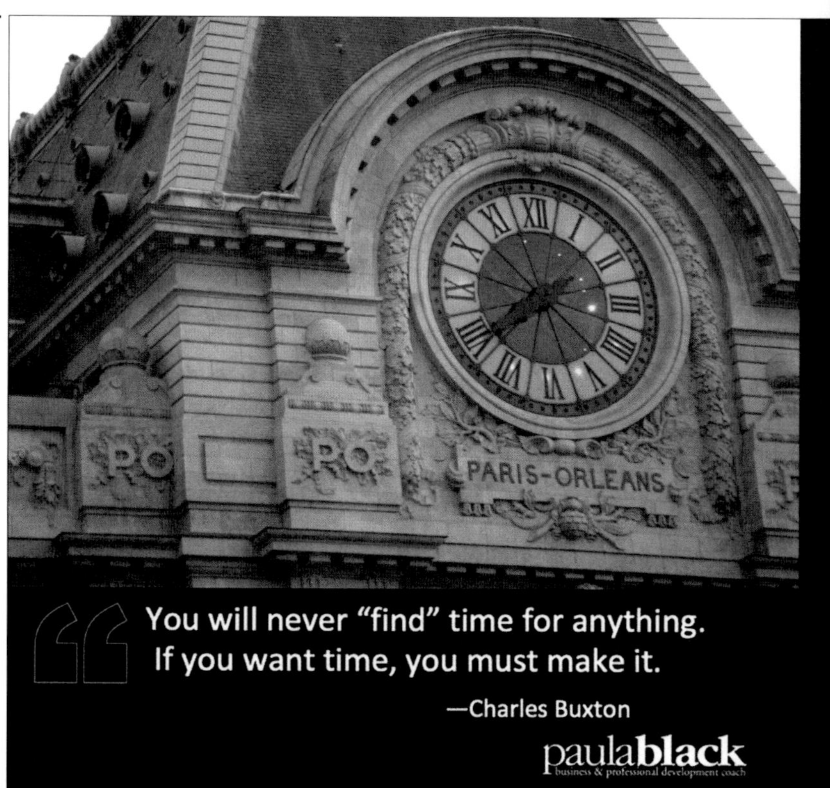

TIME—make it!

Okay. There isn't a factory someplace that manufactures TIME that is sold on Amazon.

We have to make space for it. Prioritize. Ask yourself what's really important. Then rearrange your schedule to fit your priorities. Identify what can be moved or put off to a later date, or what can be eliminated entirely, to make sure the things most important to you come first.

Remember that I could have told the New York Times I was booked that week and asked if we could do the meeting another time.

Who or what are you not prioritizing?

"Vision is the art of seeing what is invisible to others."

—Jonathan Swift

MAKE A PLAN.
COMMIT TO IT.
YOU **CAN**

HAVE WHAT
YOU WANT...
just not always
at the same time.

Be willing to see the possibilities.

ENJOY THE JOURNEY!

Focus on the journey, not the destination. Joy is found not in finishing an activity but in doing it.

—Greg Anderson

paula**black**
business & professional development coach

BE MINDFUL THAT IT'S ABOUT THE JOURNEY.

Enjoy it!

The best parts of my book, *A Lawyer's Guide to Creating a Life, Not Just a Living,* were the conversations I had with 26 lawyers and experts while creating the book.

It was NOT the satisfaction of completion or the fact that it's been an Amazon bestseller.

That is nice, BUT it was the JOURNEY that made it worthwhile—those intriguing conversations I had with 26 smart, accomplished, and insightful lawyers and experts!

FOCUS ON SOLUTIONS!

Rather than focusing on the obstacle in your path, focus on the bridge over the obstacle.

—Mary Lou Retton

paulablack
business & professional development coach

FIND THE BRIDGE.

Remember when you told your kid, "Don't drop the milk!"

They dropped the milk. YOU made them focus on the obstacle.

Focus on the solutions!

DO WHAT YOU LOVE!

"Don't waste your time with things you don't love.

—My 86-year-old mother when she was 45.

paulablack
business & professional development coach

My mother always told me,
"Don't waste your time with things you don't love;
find a way to at least like what you are doing."

And since I'm a born OPTIMIST, that philosophy
helped me LEARN to love a lot of things.

MY plan and commitment.
Denver with my 87-year-old mom:
7 years, 38 trips, 336 days, 192 movies,
11,241 precious conversations and counting.

If all of this hadn't been in place before COVID-19, it would have been an even more difficult time, my mom locked down in Denver and me in Miami. But we talked two to three times a day, as though we were in the same house TOGETHER. I sent her biographies and political books, and we talked about them during our endless conversations. On most days we watched the news, and we shared the Fourth of July festivities together, she in her den and me in mine.

If we had not had the previous seven years of developing a deep understanding of one another, the months of COVID-19 would have been superficial conversations about the weather, our health, and the family.

How deep are your conversations with the ones you love? List the people with whom you want more profound relationships.

DEFINE YOUR

OWN

SUCCESS.

Don't listen to the NAYSAYERS.

Find YOUR North Star.

Don't let anyone tell you what YOUR LIFE should look like.

Put progress over perfection.

Will you be your worst self in fear or your best self with courage?

What are the dreams that speak to YOUR soul?

DREAMS TAKE FLIGHT!

Will you ever be ready to make your dreams come true? Maybe it's not about being ready—maybe you just have to spread your wings and see what happens.

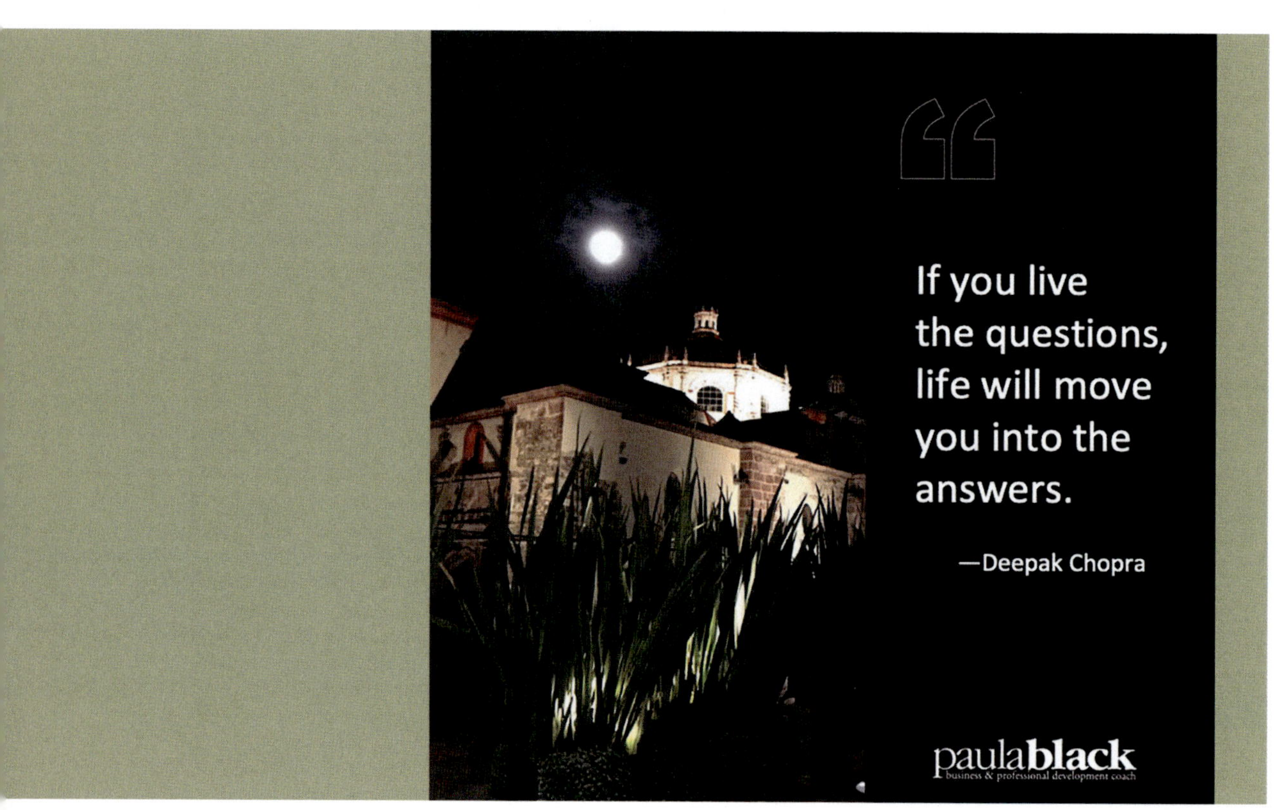
If you live
the questions,
life will move
you into the
answers.
—Deepak Chopra
paulablack
business & professional development coach

10 QUESTIONS

IT'S ABOUT MINDSET THAT WILL PRODUCE OPPORTUNITIES

1

WHAT HAS MADE YOU HAPPY OVER THE YEARS?

Really think about what has made you happy decade by decade.

A new challenge?

Interesting work?

Financial freedom?

Making a contribution to society?

Make a list of what has made you happy decade by decade.

DIG DEEP!

What will you find
in the darkness?
paulablack
business & professional development coach

Dig DEEP. They may be buried dreams.

What will you find in the darkness of your past?

What dreams did you kick to the curb when you were sucked into the pressures of building your career?

Featured in my book, *A Lawyer's Guide to Creating a Life, Not Just a Living,* is Candace Duff, a former partner at Greenberg Traurig, who kicked her dream of becoming a novelist to the curb as she climbed the ladder to partnership.

NOW she is a mediator, attorney, arbitrator, AND a three-time published NOVELIST under the pen name L.J. Taylor, her dream since she was 13 years old. Find Candace at *candaceduff.com*.

What dreams have you left in the past that should see the light of day?

2

WHAT PART OF YOUR LIFE MAKES YOU HAPPY TODAY?

Freedom.

Flexibility.

Being close to people you LOVE.

Feeling productive.

Being relevant.

Think about it. I suspect there are many things that make you happy.

List the many small things and the grandest of things.

EXAMINE THE DETAILS!

Put your heart, mind and soul into even your smallest acts. This is the secret of success.

—Swami Sivananda

If you are like some of my clients, you have found that working from home has GREAT benefits. How could you start a side gig with your newfound time?

Or if you love a particular area of what you do—how could you make a plan to do more of it?

Or if you love charity work—examine what you love about it and do more.

List your possibilities.

3

HOW CAN YOU STAY RELEVANT IN TODAY'S WORLD?

Improve your tech skills.

Understand and work with younger people.

Identify the skills and wisdom that could be adapted to today's world and people you could collaborate with to make it happen.

OWN the skills and wisdom you have to contribute.

What are the ways you will stay relevant?

LOOK AROUND!

Happiness is not a destination or an experience, it's a decision.
—Carlos Santana
paulablack
business & professional development coach

CARLOS SANTANA

exemplifies how masters can give of themselves to create cross-generational experiences—just listen to the CD *Supernatural.* You will hear how Carlos pays respect to young talent. If you listen closely you will hear them speaking to one another.

The collaboration earned them EIGHT GRAMMYS that year.

Now ask yourself who in your world YOU could engage in cross-generational conversations and collaborations at a level that will complement both of you.

You may be one of those professionals who loves what you do and want to do it until you no longer can. This is the question: How can you have your cake and eat it too? As a senior professional you have assets: experience and probably a pretty long list of clients and referral sources. You have a big Rolodex! (Yes, I remember those!) And you're probably a good rainmaker. So why not look for a young professional interested in your area of business and forge a cross-generational relationship to help build their dream while you continue yours? You just may find the joy Santana did.

Or will you just continue until it's time to turn out the lights?

This next story is paraphrased from a conversation from my book: *A Lawyer's Guide to Creating a Life, Not Just a Living.* It's a great example of a cross-generational opportunity.

Clarissa Rodriguez is a shining example of why building relationships is the key to a practice you love. She's a commercial litigator and an international arbitrator. She describes herself as becoming Indiana Jones:

Clarissa Rodriguez

I found myself taking church history courses, art classes, and getting a minor in anthropology in college. I didn't, however, become an archeologist. I became an attorney. My practice area has always been international. Miami being the hub between Latin America and Europe has afforded me the chance to work with international clients on cross-border investments, international arbitration, and litigation.

Every year, the International Law Section hosts a premier conference in Miami, titled the iLaw. The iLaw 2017 invited world-renowned attorney Donald S. Burris to be the keynote speaker. Mr. Burris's work was characterized in the movie *Woman in Gold*.

As you may know, *Woman in Gold* is a film starring Helen Mirren and Ryan Reynolds, about Holocaust survivor Maria Altmann's fight against the Austrian government to retrieve a series of Nazi-looted art taken from her family during World War II. It happens that Maria's family had commissioned the artist Gustav Klimt to paint the portrait of her aunt, Adele Bloch-Bauer. He painted what would be called *Woman in Gold*, also known as Austria's Mona Lisa. Maria Altmann's quest was to get back her family's art collection. She hired, Randy Schoenberg and Donald Burris.

The International Law Section was hosting an opening ceremony cocktail party for the iLaw conference, and I was asked to entertain Mr. Burris and his wife, a California couple in their seventies, and make them feel welcome. I was hooked. Mr. Burris and his wife invited me to dinner, and by the end of the night, I had an invitation to their home in Los Angeles. We became instant friends, and he insisted I call him Don.

Donald S. Burris

The next day, at the conference, his speech "From Tragedy to Triumph: Altmann, Benningson, and the Pursuit of Looted Art" was a splash of cold water on me. His work was impressive, inherently noble, and utterly captivating. For days I couldn't stop thinking about Don's lecture. It was an adrenaline rush.

I had a connection with Don because of our mutual passion and his area of practice. It was international, historical, and unique; it was exactly what I wanted to do.

I helped Clarissa reach out to Don and send him her thoughts on looted art cases in the news. She visited with him when she was in Los Angeles and when he was in Miami. They soon started working together to combine his expertise in looted art cases with her international law experience to pursue Cuban looted art cases. Don became of counsel to her firm, and Clarissa became his go-to Florida counsel. Their relationship benefits both of their practices and allows them to pursue new avenues that otherwise may have been too difficult or daunting. Find Clarissa and Don at *reichrodriguez.com.*

4 HOW CAN YOU MANAGE YOUR FINANCES FOR MAXIMUM FLEXIBILITY?

When the dream is COMPELLING enough,
you will FIND the financial means to make it happen.

FINANCIAL FLEXIBILITY. THE KEY!

Find a direction.

Is it up? Is it to the left or the right?

Are there guard rails or is it wide open?

Decide—then commit!

paula**black**
business & professional development coach

Financial flexibility is KEY for your THIRD ACT.

In my book, *A Lawyer's Guide to Creating a Life, Not Just a Living,* I asked John Kozyak, "How would you advise others to think about their third act?"

He said, "First, start saving early, and don't live beyond your means. I think it's obvious the government is not going to pay for a good retirement. Barbara and I have lived in the same house for the past 35 years and we've never upsized, so we don't have to downsize or pay a mortgage. As we were approaching 60, we changed financial planners. We really feel comfortable with the team we have now, and that's provided lots of comfort. I wish I had met them in my thirties." Find John at *kttlaw.com.*

What will you do to ensure your financial flexibility?

5

DO YOU WANT TO EARN AN INCOME, VOLUNTEER, OR BOTH?

KNOW YOUR REAL NEEDS!

COVID-19 opened our eyes in many ways, including what we can live without. Dinner out five nights a week. New clothes and shoes every month. A fancy car to drive—nowhere! So much of our purchasing is automatic.

During the lockdown I broke a plate from my white set of dishes. I immediately thought—I need to order a replacement! In my mother's words... ARE YOU CRAZY? I love cooking and setting an appropriate table. I have seven sets of dishes—Mexican, Italian, Chinese, and the list goes on! Not to mention my white set is a service for 12! AND I haven't had a dinner party for more than four in the past five years! Would you say that was an automatic thought to purchase something? Of course; it was certainly not a need.

What could you live without?

How could you lower your overhead?

How could you create passive income?

Now, create your plan.

ASK THE EXPERT

CASEY WEADE

is a sought-after retirement planning professional, speaker and CEO/Chief Visionary of the national financial firm, Howard Bailey. He hosts the "Retire with Purpose" radio, TV show, and podcast—providing sound financial guidance to pre-retirees and retirees across the country.

These are three excerpts from Casey's book, *Job Optional*: *The science of retiring with confidence; the art of living with purpose.*

One of the challenges I face when working with new clients is identifying the answers to these questions. The reason is because what motivates people is deeply personal and individual.

There was a study conducted in 2000 called the Cornell Retirement and Well-Being Study, which concluded that about 44 percent of retirees worked for pay after their retirement began. Did they need the money? Were they bored? Why take a job after retiring from the workforce? The answers are in what drives you personally.

The study went on to detail that, of those currently employed after retirement, 14 percent say they will "never retire" and

28 percent say they will work "as long as I am healthy." Most want their time to be filled with personal passions and new experiences.

Other reasons for returning to work after retiring:

- **Have free time – 73%**
- **Desire additional income – 63%**
- **Not ready to retire – 58%**
- **Maintain social contacts – 56%**

Retirement Red Zone. When you get within five to ten years from retirement, you reach what is often referred to as "the Retirement Red Zone." You find yourself at a point in life where the mistakes made over the coming years could make or break your retirement. As retirement specialists, most families we work with are ready to begin structuring their retirement strategy or are already in retirement and prepared to implement a real plan for their future. The sooner you take the initiative to sit with an advisor and begin planning, the greater chance you will have to retire as planned. You may feel you have plenty of time to continue to take on the risks you have in the past, but the reality may be to the contrary.

A Written Plan. Let me share with you a quick story. Maybe you've heard it before, but it's one of my favorites. Dr. Albert Einstein was traveling from New York to Chicago in the late 1920s—by train, of course. Einstein boarded the train and the conductor began passing through the cabin, collecting and punching tickets. As he approached Einstein, he noticed a concerned look on his face while shuffling through his pockets. The conductor recognized the famous doctor and told him not to worry about the ticket, as he knew he was good for it. While the conductor passed back through the cabin, he noticed Einstein still looking very disheveled, even more so than the last time he walked by. As Einstein stood on his chair looking through the luggage racks, the conductor said, "Dr. Einstein, please have a seat, we know who you are. Your ticket is really unnecessary." The concerned doctor replied, "Sir, I know who I am, the problem is I don't know where I am going!"

Based on the thousands of pre-retirees and retirees I engage with each year, I estimate that fewer than 20 percent of retirees have a written plan for retirement. That written plan is your ticket for a successful retirement—your ticket to avoid the level of concern the conductor saw on Dr. Einstein's face. When you ultimately structure a retirement strategy, it should be put in writing, so you know not only what your destination is, but also how you will get there. A retirement plan is not a stack of statements. It's not a simulation stating you have a percentage chance of success, and it's certainly not an investment strategy. A retirement plan is documentation for how each of your assets will specifically assist you in retirement. Moreover, it lays out the main risks you will face during retirement and how you will overcome them as they occur. Where will you turn in case of emergency? Where will your income come from in case of a market downturn? Where will you generate additional income in case of inflation? How will you cover potential long-term care expenses? How will you manage ongoing taxation in addition to avoiding taxes as you leave those assets behind to the next generation? Find Casey at *howardbailey.com.*

6

WHAT ARE YOUR PASSIONS AND WHAT DO YOU LONG TO DO?

Think long and hard about this!
Or maybe you're like me and
know exactly what your passions are.

TRAVEL & COOKING?

For me it's TRAVEL and COOKING! Cooking classes in Tuscany, Hong Kong, and San Miguel de Allende.

WHAT are YOU passionate about?

FAMILY & FRIENDS?

Remember that everyone needs to relax and take a break with friends!

paula**black**
business & professional development coach

YOU might love being around like-minded family and friends!

WHO are the most important people in your life?

7

WHAT'S ON YOUR LEARN-TO-DO LIST?

Learn another LANGUAGE?
Learn to play the PIANO? Write a BOOK?
Learn how to apply your private sector knowledge to public agency or non-profit work?
I'm sure your list could be long!

SOMETHING FAST?

Yes that's me. After Porsche Driving School at Homestead Miami Race Track... It was FAST, controlled, a little rainy and familiar. Oh yes, just like running a business.

At Porsche Driving School, they teach you not to look at the road directly in front of you—instead look down the road where you want to be!

That is great advice to help you figure out how you want to arrive to your THIRD ACT. I have a client who was often looking in the rearview mirror, longing for the days when he had several associates on staff and a steady flow of cases. Those days are long gone. He has slowly embraced a new road, using contract lawyers that he only pays when there is work and not having to provide them with costly overhead, office space, benefits, etc. He is now looking down the road where he wants to be—access to talented lawyers when he needs them and keeping his overhead low.

Where do you want to be?

SOMETHING WRITTEN?

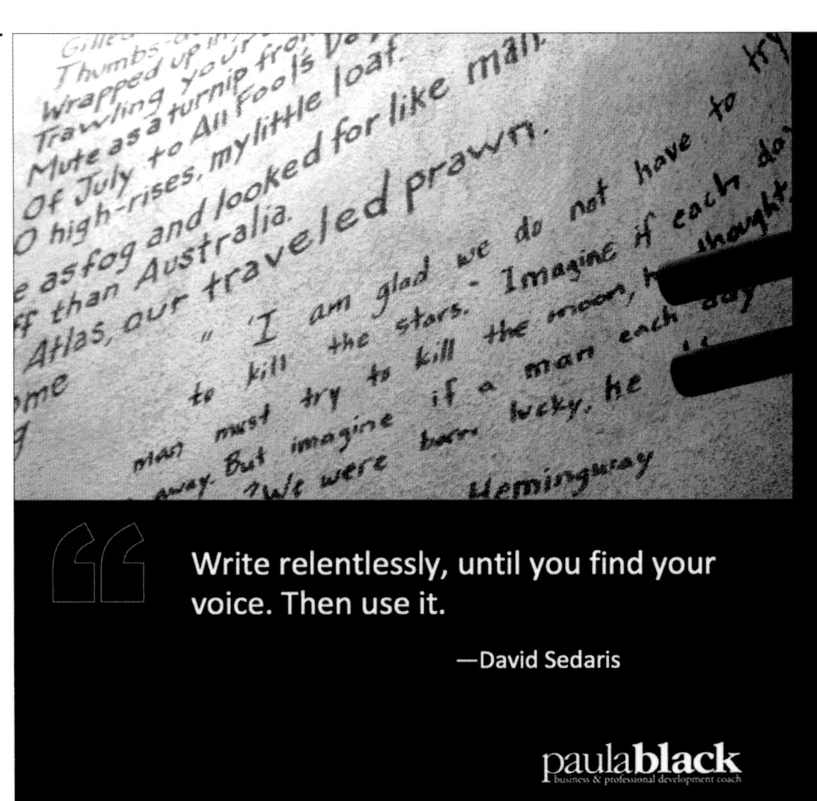

Would you like to try your hand at writing a novel, memoir, or documentary?

I have a client in his seventies who is a great storyteller and loves the written word. He is writing his boomer memoirs—his time growing up in the South, law school, the eye-opening reality of being an associate, Vietnam, etc. He will turn it into a blog where other boomers can contribute their stories. But the real power of his written words will be so that his children, grandchildren, and great-great-great-grandchildren will know who he was and where they come from—that is a worthy endeavor!

Are you a storyteller? Do you have something to say to the world?

What could you write about?
When will you start and when will you finish?

TECHNOLOGY

A while back, the Florida Bar sent out a survey about challenges facing senior lawyers. These are a tiny sampling of the responses.

What is your biggest challenge or struggle?

> Technology!
>
> Changes happen so fast it's hard to stay updated.
>
> Often I am befuddled.
>
> Technology in the courtroom.
>
> Marketing on social media platforms.
>
> Going paperless is contrary to everything I learned as a young lawyer.
>
> Competition from less qualified lawyers, because of technology-based marketing.

In my mind, there is only one explanation for this:
RESISTANCE to **CHANGE!**

You are all smart people—this isn't rocket science. If I can manage, so can YOU.

BUT you have to give up your RESISTANCE!

When it comes to technology, the problem is usually between the chair and the monitor. There is always a solution for everything else.

YOU DON'T HAVE TO DO IT ALONE!

The good news is you don't have to do it alone!

My team is 30 strong. Three IT guys, two social media specialists, an audio and video producer with lighting and audio crew—these are just a few of the talented people that help me.

Don't micromanage them. If you feel you have to, then they aren't the right fit. OR Maybe you need an ATTITUDE adjustment. I've been known to need one of those now and again!

But you should know, you do have to get them up to speed on your standards and goals.

Create a **TEAM** around you.

TEST them—start out small.

Then **LET THEM** do their job.

BE PATIENT—it will take time.

ASK THE EXPERT

CARLOS CUERVO

Photojournalist, filmmaker, and educator.

For over 16 years he has been covering stories and documenting the life of minority ethnic groups in Asia and Central and South America.

Cuervo is a consultant and speaker on the topics of video production, visual storytelling, and new media. He is an instructor at the Connecticut School of Broadcasting in Miami, Florida.

He's a passionate storyteller and believer that when it comes to telling the stories of people doing something to make a difference, there is no story too small to tell, no story too big to touch one heart and change the world for good. Find Carlos at *carloscuervo.com.*

Look like a PRO at your next Zoom meeting.

Your audience will see a reflection of the care and professionalism that you put into your setup for a Zoom meeting. Although it doesn't have to be complicated, it needs to reflect your reputation and brand.

Lighting: proper lighting separates a good image from a mediocre one. Poor lighting can make you too dark and too much light can make you too bright.

One way to make your lighting better is to do your setup close to a big window or lamp. The best results are with a big window or lamp on the side or in front of you, right behind your computer. The window should never be behind you.

The closer you are to the light source, the softer the light is and as a result, more pleasant. Be mindful that light changes throughout the day, so very early in the morning or before sunset, the light will change dramatically—fast.

Audio: Audio-visual content has elements you can see as well as elements you can hear. Many people make the mistake of only focusing on how the image looks and disregard the audio. Studies show that in communications, our human brain is more willing to forgive low quality visuals as long as the audio is clear; the opposite happens when a video has great visuals but the audio is not clear.

To enhance the audio, first look for a room or a place that is relatively quiet. Use an external microphone that can be connected to your computer. Some headsets are great for audio, but don't look great on camera. Lavaliere microphones are best for getting clear audio and are not as visible on camera.

Composition: Wide shots of your office and scenery aren't nearly as compelling as a close-up of you. Take into consideration the angle of the camera; typically you want the camera to be at eye level so you are not looking down or up at your computer. And you never want to see your ceiling. Make sure that the background is uncluttered. If there is a closet behind you, remember to close it. Make sure you don't cut off the top of your head or your shoulders.

Why? People are **watching** and **listening**!

The Supreme Court streamed live audio of arguments. And someone flushed a toilet.

The Court was holding arguments over the phone because of Covid-19, when all of a sudden there was the distinct sound of a toilet flushing, according to CNN's Supreme Court reporter Ariane de Vogue.

She writes that across the country, the public that has never before this week been able to listen in real time to oral arguments held remotely was treated not only to deep questions related to the First Amendment and robocalls but also to someone's apparent bathroom break. **Oy vey**.

TECHNOLOGY THAT WORKS FOR US!

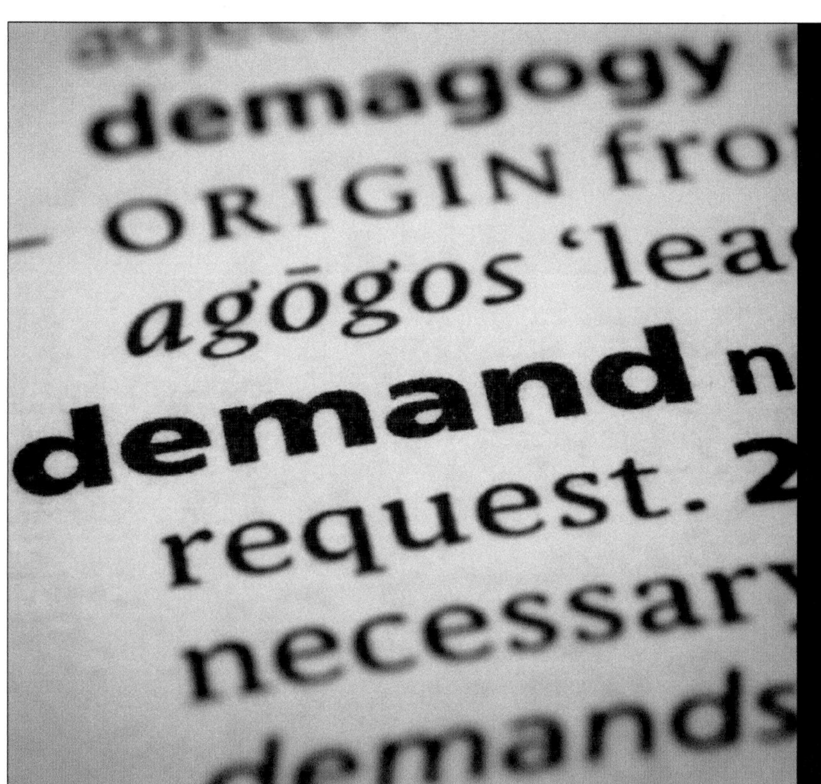

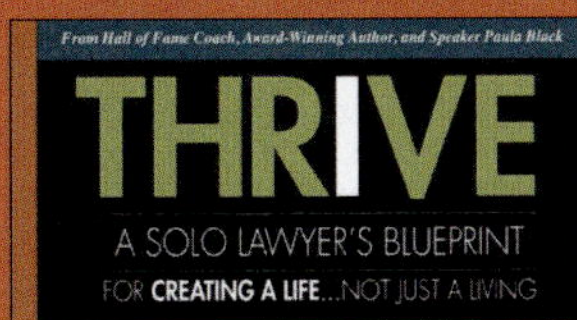

ON-DEMAND PRINTING. This makes getting a book published on Amazon so simple and cost-effective. If there is a book inside you and you would like help, shoot me an email.

SOCIAL MEDIA. It is a way of life today. There are some great benefits for all of us. Embrace what's compatible with the way you live your life. But there is one MUST do! You must have a profile on LinkedIn. EVERY professional must be reachable, and LinkedIn is the platform to use.

ONLINE COURSES. Embrace online courses for two reasons:

1. You have vast knowledge. What would make a good course that others would pay for? Like my online THRIVE course.
2. Learn from online courses. Do you know about MasterClass or The Great Courses? They are great online tools to help you figure out what you might enjoy, and you will learn a thing or two! There are courses on film, music, culinary arts, politics, writing, sports, and photography, to name a few.

STAY RELEVANT!

STOP
RESISTING CHANGE!

ASK THE EXPERT

DR. BETTY O, PHD

Entrepreneur, mom, motivational speaker, and bestselling author of the book *Fast Track to the Corner Office for Women.*

A master performance coach and certified talent consultant, Dr. Betty O coaches the top 1%. She works with Fortune 100 and 500 executives and their teams to be at the top of their game. She helps people to discover and overcome the roadblocks along the way, especially the barriers that are hiding in plain sight. What that means in real life? She is a master performance coach and personal mentor to high-potential women, celebrity clients, entrepreneurs, and executives in or on their way to the C-Suite who need someone they can trust and depend upon for insights, behavioral change, growth, and personal accountability. Find Dr. Betty O at *drbettyo.com.*

Self-Talk: Your Best Friend or Your Worst Enemy.

Being keenly aware of our "self-talk" is critical to achieving positive outcomes (happiness). In real everyday terms, the way we talk to others and ourselves instantly shapes how we perceive life, and the same perception directly impacts our behavior immediately.

Conscious, decisive self-talk is the means to take control of your life. Using strong, assertive, positive language over time, we create lasting change. We must speak in a way that is helpful, not harmful. Words determine our mindset. How we talk, think about, and perceive our surroundings are the very foundation of our reality. The goal is to create the reality you desire.

Assertive, positive self-talk is when you stake a claim for this moment of time, right here and now, instead of saying "I will" or "I am going to." There is a massive difference between "I am relentless" and "I will be relentless." Stop blaming luck. Stop blaming other people. Stop pointing to outside influences or circumstances. Stop blaming your childhood or neighborhood. Own it, be accountable to yourself, and KNOW that you have the power.

> "Your worst enemy cannot harm you as much as your own thoughts, unguarded.
>
> **—Buddha**

Control your destiny or your destiny will control you. It is entirely within our power to determine how we think and talk about life. Our problems can become a nuisance or a stepping-stone. They can hold us down or lift us up. You decide whether something is a problem or opportunity. When you miss your mark, see it as a discovery, asking what did I learn from this, as opposed to seeing it as a failure. Then, move on! Speak "Optimist" and you will not only see the difference, you will physically and psychologically feel the difference.

DR. WILLIAM J. MORTON

I know a doctor who did more in his THIRD ACT than 10 people put together! Dr. William J. Morton became a lawyer and arbitrator; got a U.S. Coast Guard captain license; loved fly fishing, astronomy, ornithology and photography; learned to play the piano; wrote two books; and became a JUDGE!

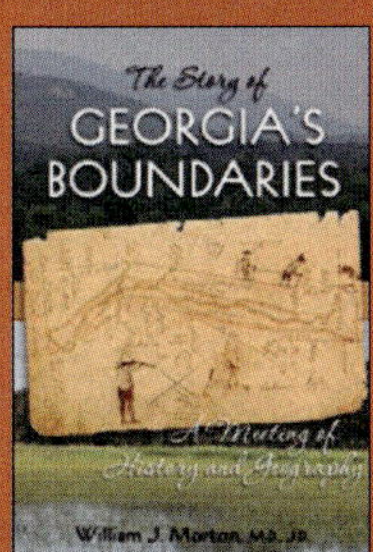

When your curiosity and drive to learn and experience more outweigh your resistance to change, your dreams will take flight!

What will you add to your bio in your THIRD ACT?

List what you will stop resisting.

____

____

____

____

____

____

____

____

List how you will stay relevant.

____

____

____

____

____

____

____

____

____

____

____

8

WHAT HAVE BEEN YOUR PROUDEST MOMENTS?

For me? It's not so much that I'm PROUD. But—THANKFUL—that I listened to the little voice in the back of my head and I made the DECISION to ACT!

HERE ARE SOME OF MY PROUDEST MOMENTS!

In 2006, my mom accompanied me to Washington, DC, to receive the Breakthrough Book of The Year Award from Independent Publishers. We had so much fun visiting all the sites in DC—the Lincoln Memorial, the Franklin Delano Roosevelt Memorial (where she sat and wept with emotion), Capitol Hill, and the National Mall. What a great opportunity to share an experience with my mom, who doesn't like to travel.

Yes, that's me! I was in Hollywood on the RED carpet after receiving the Quilly Award. The interviewer asked me my name and I couldn't answer the question! I was so excited, no blood was getting to my brain!

After my monthly meetings with Paula Black, I feel energized and focused. She helps me reset and recharge for the month, which in turn, results in higher productivity and less stress.

— Solo Estate & Wealth Planning Lawyer

I am extremely proud to be voted Best Lawyer and Law Firm Business Development Coach for three years in a row, which put me in the DBR Hall of Fame. Okay, so it's not the Hall of Fame with Mick Jagger, Stevie Nicks, and Nina Simone. But my award reconfirmed that I am doing something right. And it's making an impact!

What are YOUR proudest moments?

DECISION TO ACT!

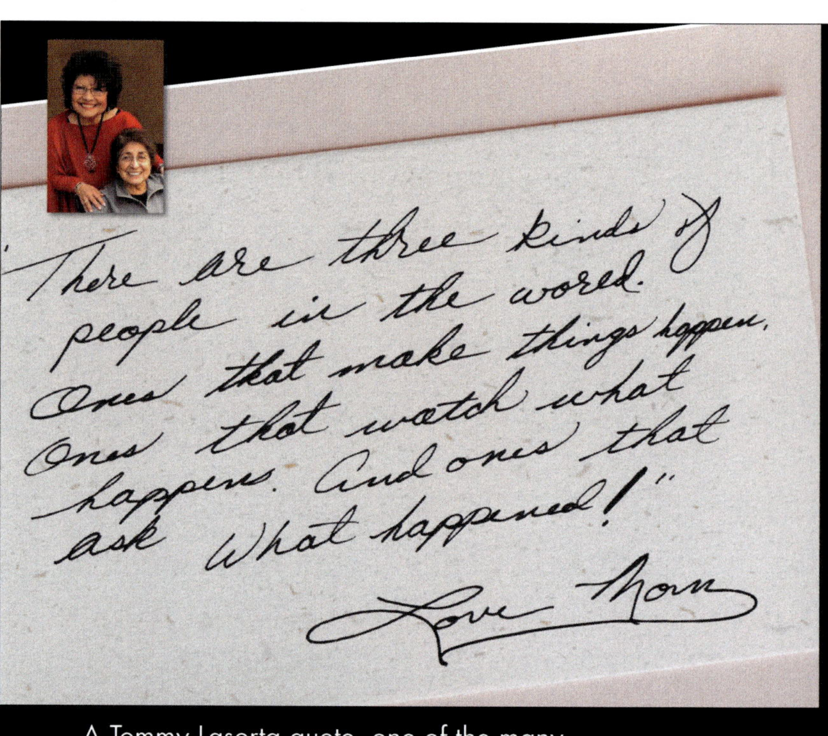

"There are three kinds of people in the world. Ones that make things happen, Ones that watch what happens. And ones that ask What happened!"

Love Mom

A Tommy Lasorta quote, one of the many inspiring quotes mom has sent me.

Take the time to really think about YOUR proudest moments.

Many of us tend to minimize our accomplishments. We often think, "That was nice... NEXT!"

So take the time to think about it and **SAVOR THOSE MOMENTS**!

Make a list of YOUR proudest moments.

9

WHAT FUELS YOUR ENERGY, ENTHUSIASM, AND JOY?

Think about the feeling of contentment you
get when you're in the ZONE,
when the endorphins are flowing!

I'm in the ZONE when I'm creating

Me and celebrity chef Rocco DiSpirito at *Miami Food and Wine Festival*

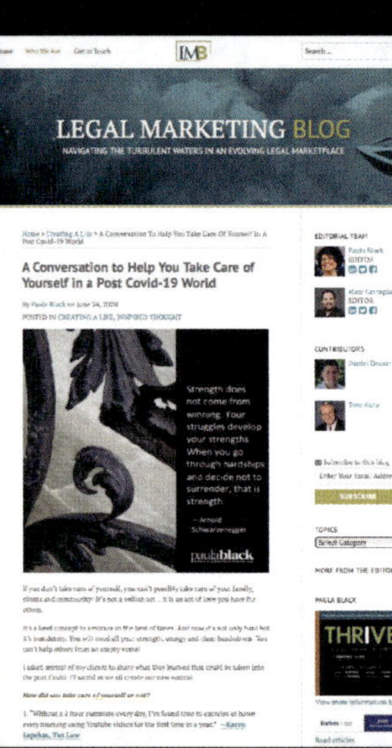

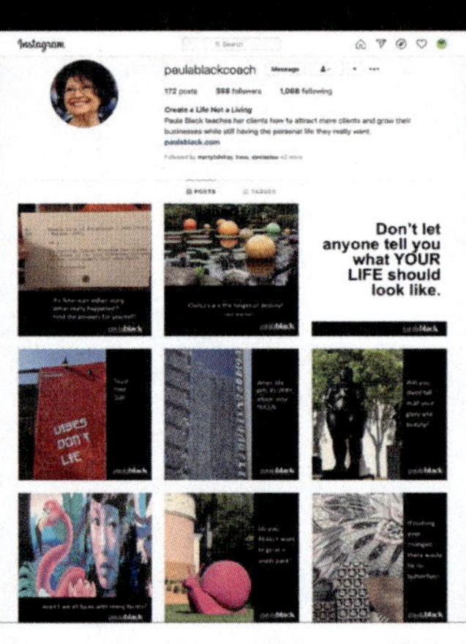

My endorphins are flowing when I'm in the zone CREATING!

When I'm cooking.

Creating an online coaching program like THRIVE.

Writing books like *A Lawyer's Guide to Creating a Life, Not Just a Living* or *The Recipe for Success* with Jack Canfield and others.

Writing and coordinating blog posts for Legal Marketing Blog.

Creating webinars and speeches.

Using my photography on Instagram.

And best of all—when I'm coaching my clients I'm in the ZONE and energized.

Make a list of what fuels YOU.

10

HOW CAN YOU TAKE CARE OF YOURSELF, SO YOU CAN ACCOMPLISH YOUR DREAMS?

Don't talk about it—take action.
Don't continually weigh the options—just pick a direction.
Don't promise to do—just do it!

THE LIST IS LONG!

Sometimes I have to remind myself to take the time to CELEBRATE my successes! This is me in Hollywood, California, at a Michelin four-star restaurant celebrating after I was on the red carpet, receiving the Quilly Award.

But I'm much more mindful when it comes to eating healthy, staying hydrated, and getting enough sleep.

How about YOU?

Maybe there are things you need to STOP doing—like drinking too much or thinking that you can hear just fine!

Self-care is not selfish—it is an act of love for those we care about.

How will you take care of yourself?

What will you stop doing?

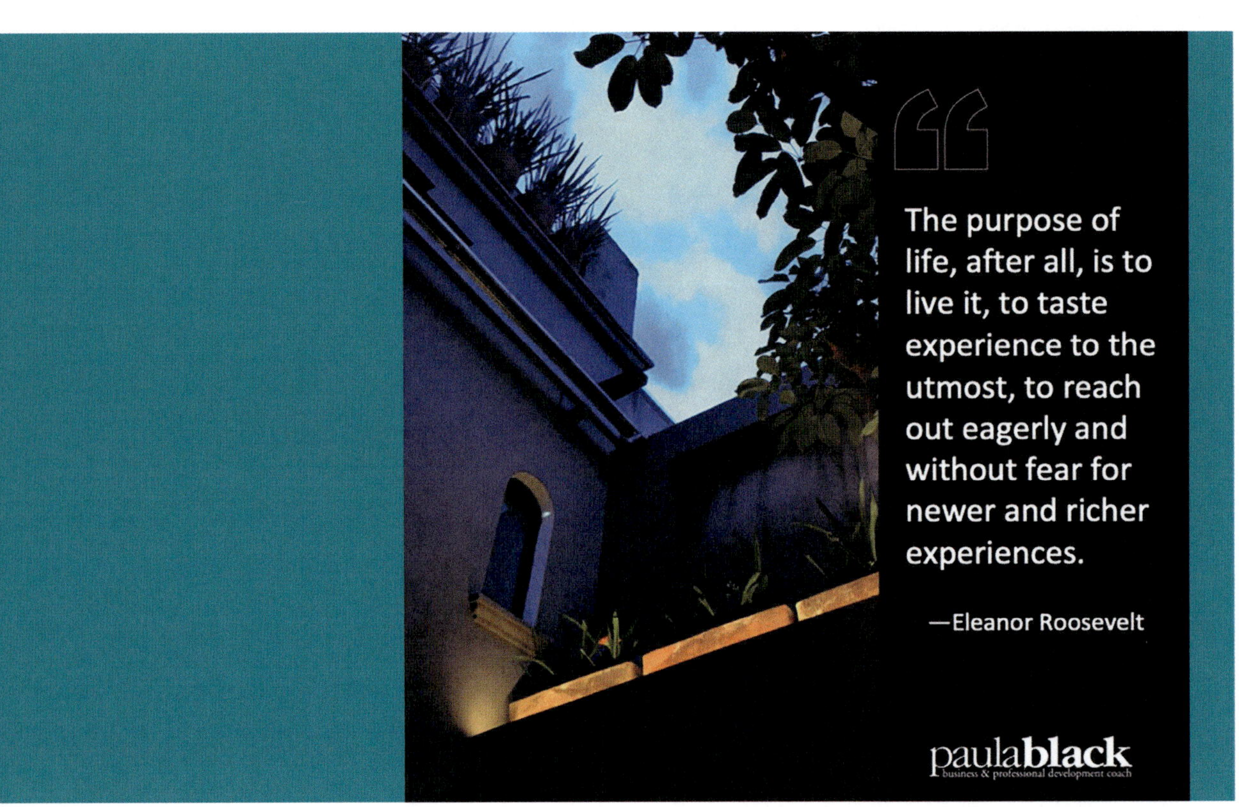
"
The purpose of life, after all, is to live it, to taste experience to the utmost, to reach out eagerly and without fear for newer and richer experiences.
—Eleanor Roosevelt
paulablack
business & professional development coach

SECTION THREE

3 TIPS

TO HELP YOU EXPLORE POSSIBILITIES

TIP 1

STOP

OVERTHINKING.

"Only those who will risk going too far can possibly find out how far one can go."

—T.S. Eliot

NO OVERTHINKING!

> I never made one of my discoveries through the process of rational thinking.
>
> —Albert Einstein

paula**black**
business & professional development coach

When you're planning your THIRD ACT, don't overthink it.
Listen to what your gut is telling you.

EACH STEP IS CLOSER!

We may not be there yet, but we're closer than we were yesterday!

paula**black**
business & professional development coach

Most of all—find JOY in the journey!

JOY WITH NO GUILT!

We have spent a lifetime doing all the things we should do, and oftentimes, doing the things we want to do make us feel guilty. I say, STOP the GUILT!

TIP 2

STAY OPEN-MINDED.

"An open mind and a willing heart are the beginning of many a great adventure. Let's get started."

—Colleen Houck, *Tiger's Dream*

WHAT WILL YOU FIND?

YOU NEVER KNOW...

If someone had told me 30 years ago that I would be coaching lawyers, I would have thought they were smoking something!

It started with two legal clients—Greenberg Traurig, when they had five offices and 350 lawyers, and Kozyak, Tropin & Throckmorton when they had little more than Kozyak, Tropin, and Throckmorton.

I had a branding and business development agency with a client base mostly in retail, media, and manufacturing. Had I not been open-minded about working with lawyers, I would have missed out on the MOST fulfilling work I have ever done in my entire career. Stay open-minded. Look at every exit as being an entrance somewhere else. You never know what you will find!

What can you be more open-minded about?

WHAT WILL YOU SEE?

WILL YOU TAKE THIS CHALLENGE?

Let's think about what Angie Lynn says, "Imagine if we treated each new dawn of each new day with the same reverence and joy as we do each new year."

I challenge YOU to treat each day with reverence and joy, with an OPEN MINDSET.

I met a gentleman at a conference; he was a coach like me. We shared stories and I told him that I do in-person coaching, to which he replied, "Oh, you are going to have to get over that in-person thing." I was polite and exited the conversation while under my breath I was fuming. "He doesn't know anything about my practice," I said to myself. "People are willing to come from various parts of the globe to work with me. I'm not going to do Zoom sessions like everyone else!"

WELL! That wasn't too open-minded, was it? Thank goodness I gave up my stubborn mindset at the end of 2019, because who knew a pandemic was around the corner? I was already a master on Zoom by March. I can see how valuable it is to be able to continue coaching even though my clients can't visit me in person.

If I could remember his name, I would thank him right here! And say I'm sorry for being so closed-minded and stubborn!

WHO WILL YOU MEET?

You may want to investigate a new environment!

Is there another area of work you've always wanted to try? Or maybe you'd like to leave a corporate role in favor of an entrepreneurial role?

I know a former state judge and private practice lawyer who, at the age of 65, took an intern position for a federal judge for a year. He loved the camaraderie and the fulfillment of doing significant work. And the federal judge loved having someone with his experience, work ethic, and dependability.

What could you be more open-minded about?

List the areas you could explore.

TIP 3

FIND

ROLE MODELS.

"We tend to become like those we admire."

—Thomas Monson

IT'S ABOUT HUNGER!

> Kobe didn't just live life—he swallowed it whole!
>
> —Rick Reilly, Sportswriter

paula**black**
business & professional development coach

For me, it is about hunger. A hunger to experience life more and more. I worry that I won't have enough time to do all the things I want to do! I love how Rick Reilly described Kobe. I challenge YOU to take giant bites and sometimes swallow life whole!

Here are MY role models:

Georgia O'Keeffe

Ruth Bader Ginsburg

"I am now 86 years old, yet people of all ages want to take their picture with me—amazing."

Marjory Stoneman Douglas

Georgia O'Keeffe: Late in life, O'Keeffe was nearly blind, but that didn't stop her. With her assistant's help, she continued to create art from her memory and vivid imagination. She died at the age of 98.

Marjory Stoneman Douglas: She died at the age of 107 and was still advocating for the Everglades in her nineties.

Ruth Bader Ginsburg: At age 86, she's still on the bench handing down decisions that affect us all. And she is vigilant about her health!

I admire these women for their tenacity, perseverance, and ability to stay relevant. My grandfather lived to 102, so I just might have longevity in my genes. I'm committed to taking care of myself, staying relevant, and continuing to be tenacious.

Who are your heroes and role models?

TAKE ACTION!

A very little key will open a very heavy door.
—Ralph Waldo Emerson
paulablack
business & professional development coach

Take action NOW. If not now, when? Thankfully I made the commitment to go home to see my mother seven years ago! That single commitment opened the door to more JOY than I could have ever imagined.

"Be **forgiving** of your past self.
Be **strict** with your present self.
Be **flexible** with your future self."

—James Clear

REMEMBER WHAT'S AT STAKE!

WHAT COULD YOUR FUTURE LOOK LIKE?

I ask you—what are you willing to commit to in order to have a fulfilling THIRD ACT? Ponder the questions and explore the possibilities you have written in this workbook. The process should be stress-free, since there are no wrong answers!

Review your lists and create your master plan.

Initiative	On a scale of 1-10 how important is it in your life? (1 being highest)	Start & Finish Date

"When one door closes, another opens; but we often look so long and so regretfully upon the closed door that we do not see one which has opened for us."

—**Alexander Graham Bell**

A Few Last Words

We have all spent a lifetime struggling to be successful, doing what we thought we should do in order to get there, making sacrifices big and small. We have found success and some of us have never let ourselves feel the euphoria of success for fear it might be fleeting or because we simply didn't make the time.

Now that we are older and wiser, we can put all of that behind us and create a path that will be of our own making with a new objective to be happy and add more joy and fulfillment to our THIRD ACT. It won't be easy, because we will have to think differently than we have ever done before. I hope my journey has inspired you to reinvent your life and retirement. If you'd like an added perspective, I would love to help you find your unique path. I am creative and often see opportunities that others may overlook, and I know how to connect the dots to make them happen. Since I've been coaching high-level clients for decades, I've developed a finely tuned "gut" to recognize pitfalls and cliffs to avoid. Feel free to email me to see how I can help you achieve your dreams: *paula@paulablack.com.*

Notes

Made in the USA
Columbia, SC
30 August 2020

18650770R00093